Easy Soup RECIPES

Delicious Soups to Warm Your ♥

Cookbook Resources, LLC
Highland Village, Texas

Easy Soup Recipes
Delicious Soups to Warm Your Heart

1st Printing - April 2010

© Copyright 2010 by Cookbook Resources, LLC

International Standard Book Number: 978-1-59769-044-7

Library of Congress Control Number: 2010005787

Library of Congress Cataloging-in-Publication Data

     Easy soup recipes.
        p. cm.
     Includes index.
     ISBN 978-1-59769-044-7
     1. Soups. 2. Stews. 3. Quick and easy cookery. I. Cookbook Resources, LLC. II. Title.
     TX757.E283 2010
     641.8'13--dc22

                             2010005787

Cover and Design by Nancy Bohanan

Edited, Designed and Published in the United States of America and Manufactured in China by
Cookbook Resources, LLC
541 Doubletree Drive
Highland Village, Texas 75077

Toll free 866-229-2665

www.cookbookresources.com

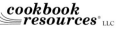

cookbook resources LLC

Bringing Family and Friends to the Table

Warm Your Heart

There's nothing quite like soup. It seems to provide a sense of wellness and comfort unlike any other food we eat. Soup has a way of making us feel better when we're sick and safer when we're vulnerable or insecure.

In its own way, soup seems to wrap its arms around us to say, "Everything's going to be okay. Just relax, calm down and sip a spoonful of these wonderful flavors."

Besides its medicinal and emotional benefits, soup is so easy that we sometimes forget just how easy and convenient it can be. When you are in a rush and you've been fighting traffic and rain, it is easy to come home, open a can of soup, add some frozen vegetables, maybe some leftovers and seasonings, and have a great tasting dish that seems to make the day's stresses go away.

Even kids will eat soup. You may have to puree the vegetables to hide them, but they usually like the warmth and healing qualities of soup even though they may not "understand" all the benefits of soup.

They'll remember when Monday night was soup night and the whole family sat at the table. They'll remember when everyone talked about what happened that day and what was ahead of them for the rest of the week.

The little things, like sharing a meal at the table, are more important than we realize. These little things are really the big things we never forget.

Have a bowl of soup. Relax, everything's going to be okay.

Contents

Soups

Cold Soups

Chicken Soups

Turkey Soups

Beef Soups

Pork Soups

Seafood Soups

Contents

Soups – continued

Stews, Chilis and Chowders

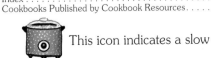 This icon indicates a slow cooker recipe.

Fresh Avocado Soup

3 ripe avocados
¼ cup fresh lemon juice
1 (10 ounce) can chicken broth
1 (8 ounce) carton plain yogurt
Chopped chives

- Peel avocados, remove seeds and cut into pieces. Immediately put avocados, lemon juice, broth and yogurt into blender and process until smooth.

- Add a little salt and pepper and refrigerate for several hours. Serve in soup bowls with chopped chives on top. Serves 4 to 6.

Check seasonings of cold soups just before serving because chilled foods tend to dull the taste buds and will need more seasoning than hot soups.

Artichoke for Grins

3 tablespoons butter
2 tablespoons finely minced green onions
1½ tablespoons flour
2 (14 ounce) cans chicken broth
1 (16 ounce) can artichoke bottoms, drained
1 cup half-and-half cream

- Melt butter in large saucepan and saute green onions. Stir in flour and cook for 3 minutes. Slowly add broth, stir constantly and cook on medium heat until mixture thickens.

- Puree artichokes in blender and stir into broth mixture with a little salt and pepper. Add half-and-half cream and heat just until soup is thoroughly hot.

- This soup may be served hot or cold. If serving cold, do not heat after adding cream. Refrigerate for 2 hours before serving. Serves 6.

Customer: Waiter, this soup tastes funny.

Waiter: So why aren't you laughing?

Sweet Carrot Soup

1 (16 ounce) package shredded carrots
1 cup orange juice
1 cup apricot nectar
¼ cup lemon juice
⅓ cup honey
⅓ cup sour cream

- Combine carrots, orange juice, apricot nectar and ½ cup water in large saucepan. Cook on high until almost boiling, reduce heat and simmer for 20 minutes.

- Add lemon juice, honey and sour cream and stir well. Serve soup at room temperature or chilled. Serves 6.

To keep cold soups chilled for a longer time, put bowls in the refrigerator or freezer before pouring soup and serving.

Chilled Summertime Soup

3 cups chilled, cubed fresh cantaloupe, divided
3 cups chilled, cubed fresh honeydew melon
2 cups chilled, fresh orange juice
2 cups chilled white wine or champagne
¼ cup chilled, fresh lime juice
3 tablespoons honey

- Puree 2 cups cantaloupe in food processor or blender and pour into large bowl. Puree honeydew melon and combine with pureed cantaloupe, orange juice, white wine and lime juice.

- Pour in honey and mix well. Chop remaining cantaloupe and add to bowl. Serve immediately. Serves 8.

TIP: Fresh mint as garnish is always a nice touch.

The earliest archaeological evidence of humans eating soup dates back 6000 BC. The soup was hippopotamus soup.

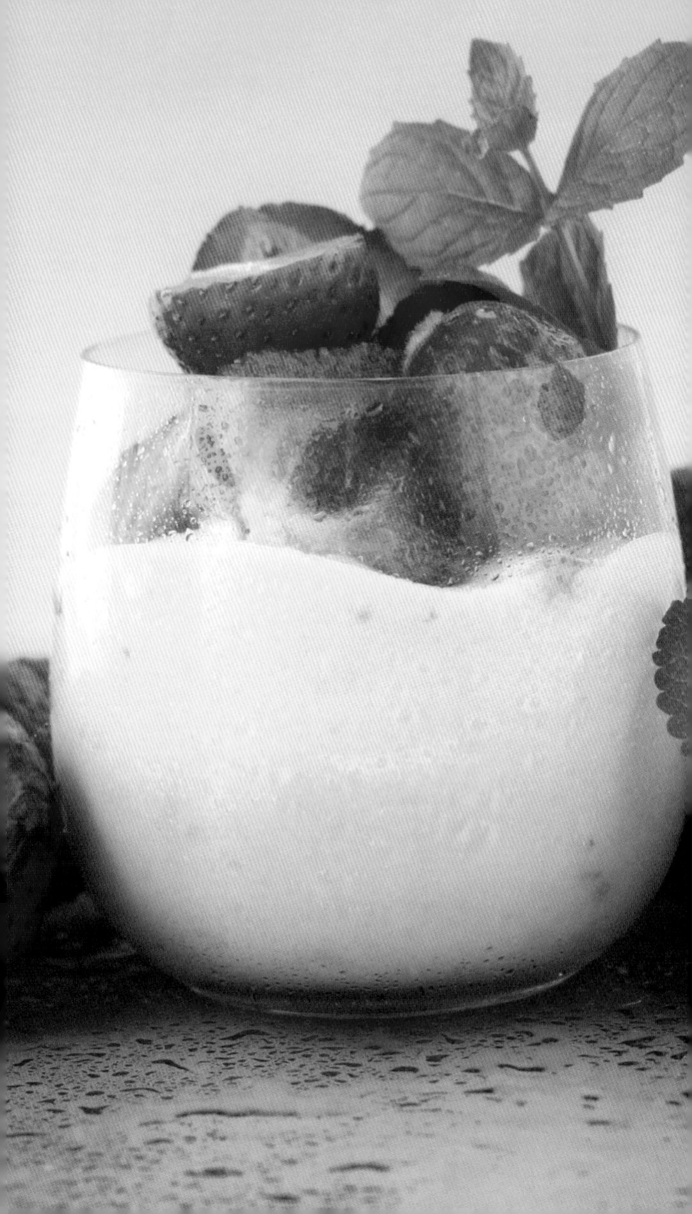

Cold Strawberry Soup

2¼ cups strawberries
⅓ cup sugar
½ cup sour cream
½ cup whipping cream
½ cup light red wine

- Puree strawberries and sugar in blender. Add sour cream and whipping cream and blend well.

- Pour into pitcher. Add red wine and 1¼ cups water. Stir and refrigerate before serving. Serves 4 to 6.

Cold soups have been served since the beginning of mankind. They hydrate the body and contain salt and other seasonings, garlic and wine vinegar as examples, that have some medicinal qualities.

Rio Grande Gazpacho

This spicy, nutritious vegetable soup made from a puree of raw vegetables is served cold and is great in the summer.

1 cucumber, peeled, seeded, quartered
½ onion, quartered
1 teaspoon minced garlic
3¼ cups tomato juice, divided
1 pound tomatoes, peeled, quartered, cored
3 tablespoons red wine vinegar
1 tablespoon olive oil
½ teaspoon ground cumin
2 teaspoons hot sauce

- Combine cucumber, onion, garlic, and 2 cups tomato juice in blender.

- Process until vegetables are coarsely chopped. Add tomatoes and process again until vegetables are finely chopped.

- Pour into medium container with tight lid. Stir in wine vinegar, olive oil, ½ teaspoon salt, cumin, and hot sauce.

- Stir in remaining tomato juice, cover and refrigerate for 24 hours. Serve cold. Serves 6.

Creamy Cucumber Soup

2 seedless cucumbers, peeled, coarsely chopped
2 green onions, coarsely chopped
1 tablespoon lemon juice
1 (1 pint) carton half-and-half cream
1 (8 ounce) carton sour cream
1 teaspoon dried dill weed

- Process cucumbers, onions and lemon juice in blender until mixture is smooth. Transfer pureed mixture to bowl with lid.

- Gently stir in half-and-half cream, sour cream, dill weed, 1 teaspoon salt and ½ teaspoon pepper.

- Cover and refrigerate for several hours before serving. Stir mixture well before serving in soup bowls. Serves 6.

An old Yiddish saying affirms what we already know: "Troubles are easier to take with soup than without."

Tortellini Soup

1 (1 ounce) packet white sauce mix
3 boneless, skinless chicken breast halves
1 (14 ounce) can chicken broth
1 teaspoon minced garlic
1 tablespoon dried basil
1 (8 ounce) package cheese tortellini
1½ cups half-and-half cream
1 (10 ounce) package fresh baby spinach

- Place white sauce mix in sprayed 5 to 6-quart slow cooker. Add 4 cups water and stir until mixture is smooth.

- Cut chicken into 1-inch pieces. Add chicken, broth, garlic, basil, 1 teaspoon salt and 1 teaspoon pepper to mixture.

- Cover and cook on LOW for 6 to 7 hours or on HIGH for 3 hours.

- Stir in tortellini, cover and cook 1 hour more on HIGH. Stir in half-and-half cream and fresh spinach and cook just enough for soup to get hot. Serves 6.

La Placita Enchilada Soup

6 boneless, skinless chicken breast halves
½ cup (1 stick) butter
2 cloves garlic, minced
1 onion, minced
⅓ cup flour
1 (15 ounce) can Mexican stewed tomatoes,
    chopped
1 (7 ounce) can diced green chilies
1 (1 pint) carton sour cream
1 (8 ounce) package shredded cheddar cheese

- Cook chicken with 12 cups water in large saucepan until tender. Reserve broth, cube chicken and set aside. Melt butter in large roasting pan and cook garlic and onion until tender.

- Add 1 teaspoon salt to flour in bowl, slowly pour flour into butter mixture and stir constantly to dissolve all lumps.

- Continue stirring and slowly pour in reserved chicken broth. Cook until soup thickens to desired consistency.

- Add chicken, tomatoes, green chilies and sour cream. Mix well and heat. Serve in individual bowls and sprinkle with cheese. Serves 6.

Chicken and Rice Mambo Gumbo

3 (14 ounce) cans chicken broth
1 pound boneless, skinless chicken
    breasts, cubed
2 (15 ounce) cans whole kernel corn, drained
2 (15 ounce) cans stewed tomatoes with liquid
3/4 cup white rice
2 tablespoons Cajun seasoning
2 (10 ounce) packages frozen okra, thawed,
    chopped

- Combine chicken broth and chicken in soup pot
  and cook on high heat for 15 minutes.

- Add remaining ingredients and 1 teaspoon
  pepper and bring to boil Reduce heat and
  simmer for 30 minutes or until rice is done.
  Serves 8.

> You can give canned broth
> a little extra flavor by
> simmering reserved chicken or
> meat bones in the broth for
> 15 minutes. Strain the liquid
> and use it for your soup.

Quick Chicken-Noodle Soup

2 (14 ounce) cans chicken broth
2 boneless, skinless chicken breast
    halves, cubed
1 (8 ounce) can sliced carrots, drained
2 ribs celery, sliced
½ (8 ounce) package medium egg noodles

- Combine broth, chicken, carrots, celery and generous dash of pepper in large saucepan. Boil and cook for 3 minutes.

- Stir in noodles, reduce heat and cook for 10 minutes or until noodles are done; stir often. Serves 4 to 6.

Chicken noodle soup is the most popular soup.

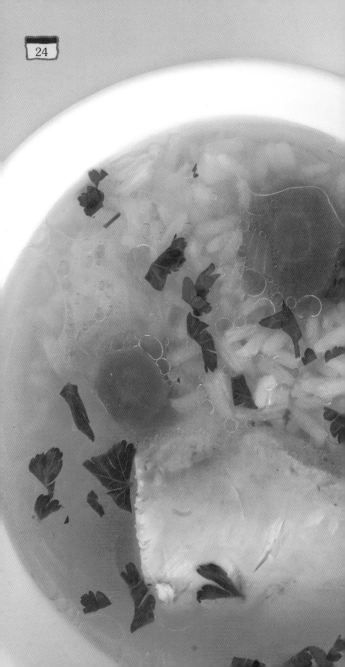

Easy Chicken-Rice Soup

**8 boneless, skinless chicken breast
    halves, cooked
2 (14 ounce) cans chicken broth
1 cup sliced carrots
1 cup rice**

- Cut cooked chicken into small pieces and place in large saucepan.

- Add chicken broth, carrots, rice, 1 teaspoon salt and ¼ teaspoon pepper and simmer for about 35 minutes or until rice is tender. Serves 6.

A team of scientists at the University of Nebraska confirmed what grandmothers have known for centuries - chicken soup is good for colds. Chicken soup contains several anti-inflammatory ingredients that affect the immune system.

Pepe's Tortilla Soup

*Don't let the number of ingredients keep
you from serving this. It's really easy.*

**3 large boneless, skinless chicken breast halves,
     cooked, cubed**
1 (10 ounce) package frozen corn, thawed
1 onion, chopped
3 (14 ounce) cans chicken broth
**2 (10 ounce) cans diced tomatoes and
     green chilies**
2 teaspoons ground cumin
2 teaspoons chili powder
1 clove garlic, minced
6 corn tortillas

- Combine all ingredients except tortillas in
  large soup pot. Bring to boil, reduce heat and
  simmer for 35 minutes.

- Preheat oven to 350°.

- While soup simmers, cut tortillas into 1-inch
  strips and place on baking sheet. Bake for
  about 5 minutes or until crisp. Serve tortilla
  strips with each serving of soup. Serves 6.

Zesty Creamy Chicken Soup

Can you open cans? Don't be put off by the number of ingredients in this recipe.

2 tablespoons butter
½ onion, finely chopped
1 (10 ounce) can cream of mushroom soup
2 (10 ounce) cans cream of chicken soup
1 (14 ounce) can chicken broth
2 soup cans milk
1 (16 ounce) package, cubed Mexican Velveeta® cheese
4 boneless, skinless chicken breast halves, cooked, diced

- Melt butter in large saucepan or roasting pan and saute onion for 10 minutes, but do not brown. Add remaining ingredients and heat but do not boil.

- Reduce heat to low, cook until cheese melts and stir constantly. Serve piping hot. Serves 8.

TIP: This is really the "easy" way to make chicken soup and if you are in an absolute rush, you could even use 2 (12 ounce) cans chicken. Leftover turkey could be substituted for chicken.

Chicky Soup

1½ - 2 pounds boneless, skinless chicken thighs
1 (16 ounce) package frozen stew vegetables
1 (1 ounce) packet dry vegetable soup mix
1¼ cups pearl barley
2 (14 ounce) cans chicken broth

- Combine all ingredients plus 1 teaspoon each of salt and pepper and 4 cups water in sprayed large slow cooker.

- Cover and cook on LOW for 5 to 6 hours or on HIGH for 3 hours. Serves 6.

> Slow cookers usually have two temperature settings: LOW is about 200° and HIGH is about 300°. When the heating elements are in the sides, food is cooked on all sides and does not have to be stirred. When the heating element is in the bottom, it is best to stir the food once or twice. Increase cooking time by 15 to 20 minutes each time the lid is removed.

Confetti Chicken Soup

1 pound boneless, skinless chicken thighs
1 (6 ounce) package chicken and
**   herb-flavored rice**
3 (14 ounce) cans chicken broth
3 carrots, peeled, sliced
1 (10 ounce) can cream of chicken soup
1½ tablespoons chicken seasoning
1 (10 ounce) package frozen corn, thawed
1 (10 ounce) package frozen baby green
**   peas, thawed**

- Cut thighs in thin strips.

- Combine chicken, rice, chicken broth, carrots, soup, chicken seasoning and 1 cup water in sprayed 5 to 6-quart slow cooker.

- Cover and cook on LOW for 8 to 9 hours.

- About 30 minutes before serving, turn heat to HIGH and add corn and peas to cooker. Continue cooking for additional 30 minutes. Serves 6.

Creamy Chicken-Spinach Soup

1 (9 ounce) package refrigerated cheese tortellini
2 (14 ounce) cans chicken broth, divided
1 (10 ounce) can cream of chicken soup
1 (12 ounce) can white chicken meat with liquid
1 (10 ounce) package frozen chopped spinach
2 cups milk

- Cook tortellini in soup pot with 1 can chicken broth according to package directions.

- Stir in remaining can broth, soup, chicken, spinach, milk, 1 teaspoon salt and ½ teaspoon pepper. Bring to boil, reduce heat to low and simmer for 10 minutes. Serves 8.

Canned soups are very convenient and many times can be improved by adding fresh ingredients, seasonings and leftovers.

Steaming Broccoli-Rice Soup

1 (6 ounce) package chicken and wild rice mix
1 (10 ounce) package frozen chopped broccoli
2 (10 ounce) cans cream of chicken soup
1 (12 ounce) can chicken breast chunks

- Combine rice mix, contents of seasoning packet and 5 cups water in soup pot. Bring to boil, reduce heat and simmer for 15 minutes.

- Stir in broccoli, chicken soup and chicken. Cover and simmer for additional 5 minutes. Serves 8.

Frozen vegetables take less time to cook than fresh vegetables. When you are in a hurry, frozen vegetables are the way to go.

Cold Night Bean Dinner

1½ cups dried navy beans
3 (14 ounce) cans chicken broth
4 tablespoons (½ stick) butter
1 onion, chopped
1 clove garlic, minced
3 cups chopped, cooked chicken
1½ teaspoons ground cumin
2 teaspoons cayenne pepper
Shredded Monterey Jack cheese

- Sort, wash beans and place in soup pot. Cover with water 2 inches above beans and soak overnight.

- Drain beans and add broth, butter, 1 cup water, onion and garlic. Bring to boil, reduce heat and cover. Simmer for 2 hours and stir occasionally. Add more water if needed.

- With potato masher, mash half beans. Add chicken, cumin and cayenne pepper. Bring to boil, reduce heat and cover. Simmer for additional 30 minutes.

- When ready to serve, spoon in bowls and top with 1 to 2 tablespoons cheese. Serves 8.

Oriental Chicken-Noodle Soup

**1 (3 ounce) package chicken-flavor ramen
noodles**
1 rotisserie chicken, boned, skinned, cubed
**2 medium stalks bok choy with leaves,
thinly sliced**
1 (8 ounce) can sliced carrots, drained
1 red bell pepper, seeded, chopped

- Break apart noodles, place in 3 cups water and heat in soup pot. Stir in chicken, bok choy, carrots and bell pepper.

- Bring to boil, reduce heat and simmer for 3 minutes; stir occasionally. Stir in flavor packet from noodles and serve immediately. Serves 8.

More than 50% of all
chicken soup consumed
is sold during the cold and
flu seasons.

Turkey-Tortilla Soup

This is a great day-after-Thanksgiving meal.

2 (14 ounce) cans chicken broth
2 (15 ounce) cans Mexican stewed tomatoes
1 (16 ounce) package frozen succotash, thawed
      or leftover vegetables
2 teaspoons chili powder
1 teaspoon dried cilantro
2 cups crushed tortilla chips, divided
2½ cups cooked, chopped turkey

- Combine broth, tomatoes, succotash, chili powder, cilantro, ⅓ cup crushed tortilla chips and turkey in sprayed large slow cooker and stir well.

- Cover and cook on LOW for 3 to 5 hours. When ready to serve, sprinkle remaining chips over each serving. Serves 6.

TIP: Just to let you know, smoked turkey is just not as good as roasted turkey for this soup.

Gobbler Special

¼ cup (½ stick) butter
1 onion, chopped
3 ribs celery, finely chopped
2 (14 ounce) cans turkey broth
1 (6 ounce) box roasted-garlic long grain-wild
     rice mix
2 (10 ounce) cans cream of chicken soup
2 cups cooked, diced white meat turkey
1 cup milk

- Melt butter in soup pot over medium heat. Add onion and celery and cook for 10 minutes.

- Add turkey broth, 1½ cups water and rice and bring to boil Reduce heat and cook on low for about 15 minutes or until rice is tender.

- Stir in chicken soup, turkey, milk and ¾ teaspoon pepper. Stir constantly and cook on medium heat until mixture is thoroughly hot. Serves 6.

*Cut loss; don't toss.
Bits of leftovers can easily go into soups, stews, stir-fry, sandwiches, etc., later in the week.*

Smoked Turkey Stampede

2 tablespoons olive oil
1 small onion, chopped
1 green bell pepper, seeded, chopped
1 (14 ounce) can chicken broth
1 medium potato, peeled, cubed
1 pound smoked turkey kielbasa, sliced
1 (15 ounce) can great northern beans
    with liquid

- Combine oil, onion and bell pepper in soup pot and cook for 5 minutes. Stir in broth, potato, turkey kielbasa, 1 cup water and a little salt and pepper.

- Bring to boil, reduce heat to medium and simmer for 15 minutes or until potato is tender.

- Stir in beans and heat just until soup is thoroughly hot. Serves 6.

Customer: Waiter, I can't seem to find any oysters in this oyster soup.

Waiter: "Well, you won't find angels in the angel food cake either, sir."

Hearty 15-Minute Turkey Soup

This is great served with cornbread.

1 (14 ounce) can chicken broth
3 (15 ounce) cans navy beans with liquid
1 (28 ounce) can Italian stewed tomatoes
   with liquid
3 cups cooked, cubed white turkey
2 teaspoons minced garlic
1 (6 ounce) package baby spinach, stems
   removed

- Combine broth, beans, stewed tomatoes, turkey, garlic and a little salt and pepper in soup pot.

- Bring to boil, reduce heat and simmer on medium heat for about 10 minutes.

- Stir in baby spinach, boil and cook, stirring constantly for 5 minutes. Serves 8.

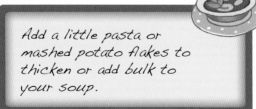

Add a little pasta or mashed potato flakes to thicken or add bulk to your soup.

Turkey with Avocado

3 large potatoes, peeled, cubed
2 (14 ounce) cans chicken broth
1 teaspoon ground thyme
½ pound smoked turkey breast, cubed
1 (10 ounce) package frozen corn
3 slices bacon, cooked crisp, drained
1 large avocado
4 plum tomatoes, coarsely chopped
1 lime

- Combine potatoes, broth and thyme in soup pot, cover and bring to boil Reduce heat and simmer until potatoes are tender, for about 20 minutes.

- With slotted spoon transfer half of potatoes to blender or food processor, puree and pour into soup pot. Add turkey and corn and simmer for 5 minutes.

- Crumble bacon; peel and slice avocado. Add bacon, avocado, tomatoes, juice of lime and a little salt and pepper to turkey mixture. Stir gently to mix. Serves 8.

TIP: Peel and cut avocado just before serving to prevent discoloration.

Tasty Turkey-Veggie Brew

2 (14 ounce) cans chicken broth
2 teaspoons minced garlic
1 (16 ounce) package frozen corn
1 (10 ounce) package frozen cut green beans
1 (10 ounce) package frozen sliced carrots
2 (15 ounce) cans Italian stewed tomatoes
2½ cups cooked, cubed turkey
1 cup shredded mozzarella cheese

- Combine broth, 1 cup water, garlic, corn, green beans, carrots, tomatoes, turkey and 1 teaspoon salt in large, heavy soup pot.

- Bring to boil, reduce heat and simmer for 15 minutes. Before serving, top each bowl of soup with mozzarella cheese. Serves 8.

The first carrots were white, yellow and purple. People in the Netherlands changed the color to orange to match their national color.

Cream of Turkey Blend

1 (10 ounce) can cream of celery soup
1 (10 ounce) can cream of chicken soup
2 soup cans milk
1 cup cooked, finely diced turkey

- Combine all ingredients in large saucepan.

- Serve hot. Serves 4.

The Campbell Soup
Company began in 1868 as a
canning company. One of its
chemist/owners developed
condensed soup in 1897 and it
won a gold medal at the Paris
Exposition in 1900. The medal
insignia continues to be on its
labels today.

Turkey Tango

3 - 4 cups chopped turkey
2 (14 ounce) cans chicken broth
2 (10 ounce) cans diced tomatoes and
    green chilies
1 (15 ounce) can whole kernel corn, drained
1 large onion, chopped
1 (10 ounce) can tomato soup
3 tablespoons cornstarch

- Combine turkey, broth, tomatoes and green chilies, corn, onion and tomato soup in large roasting pan.

- Mix cornstarch with 3 tablespoons water and add to soup mixture.

- Bring mixture to a boil, reduce heat and simmer for 2 hours. Stir occasionally. Serves 6 to 8.

> If you have any leftover cooked pasta, meat or vegetables, use them for soup ingredients. Most cooked vegetables can also be pureed and stirred in to thicken soups.

Fresh Beefy Vegetable Soup

1 pound lean ground beef
1 onion, chopped
1 (15 ounce) can Italian stewed tomatoes
1 (8 ounce) can whole kernel corn
1 large potato, peeled, cubed
1 carrot, thinly sliced
2 (14 ounce) cans beef broth
2 tablespoons flour

- Brown beef and onion in large, heavy soup pot over medium heat. Add stewed tomatoes, corn, potato, carrot, beef broth and 2 cups water. Bring to boil, reduce heat and simmer for 1 hour.

- Combine flour and ¼ cup water in bowl and stir to make paste. On medium heat, add paste to soup with a little salt and pepper and cook, stirring constantly until soup thickens. Serves 6 to 8.

TIPS: For an extra "kick", sprinkle hot sauce on top of individual bowls of soup.

This is a great recipe for leftovers. If you've got a leftover vegetable in the refrigerator, throw it in the pot!

Italian Beefy Veggie Soup

1 pound lean ground beef
2 (15 ounce) cans Italian stewed tomatoes
2 (14 ounce) cans beef broth
2 teaspoons Italian seasoning
1 (16 ounce) package frozen mixed vegetables
⅓ cup shell macaroni
1 (8 ounce) package shredded Italian cheese

- Cook beef in large soup pot for 5 minutes. Stir in tomatoes, broth, 1 cup water, seasoning, mixed vegetables, macaroni and a little salt and pepper.

- Bring to boil, reduce heat and simmer for 10 to 15 minutes or until macaroni is tender.

- Ladle into individual serving bowls and sprinkle several tablespoons cheese over top of soup. Serves 8.

TIP: *Great for leftover roast, flat-iron steak or pot roasts.*

When is soup musical?
When it's piping hot.

Southwestern Round-Up

1½ pounds lean ground beef
2 (15 ounce) cans pinto beans with liquid
1 (15 ounce) can ranch-style (chili) beans,
    drained
2 (15 ounce) cans whole kernel corn with liquid
2 (15 ounce) cans Mexican stewed tomatoes
2 (1 ounce) packets taco seasoning

- Brown beef in large soup pot, stir until beef
  crumbles and drain. Add beans, corn, tomatoes
  and 1½ cups water.

- Bring to boil, reduce heat and stir in taco
  seasoning. Simmer for 25 minutes. Serves 8.

The Indians who lived in
the New World and Mexico
used chile peppers, beans,
corn and squash in most
of their dishes. These
ingredients have developed
into a regional cuisine that
is known around the world.

Kitchen-Sink Taco Soup

1¼ pounds lean ground beef
1 onion, chopped
1 (.04 ounce) packet ranch dressing mix
2 (15 ounce) cans black beans with liquid
1 (15 ounce) can whole kernel corn with liquid
1 (15 ounce) can cream-style corn
3 (15 ounce) cans Mexican stewed tomatoes
with liquid

- Brown ground beef and onion in skillet, drain and stir in ranch dressing mix.

- Combine beef-onion mixture, beans, corn, cream-style corn and stewed tomatoes in roasting pan.

- Bring to boil, lower heat and simmer for 10 to 15 minutes. Serves 6.

TIP: Serve over tortilla chips and sprinkle with cheese.

What do ducks have for lunch?

Soup and quackers!

Chunky Beefy Noodles

1 pound beef round steak, cubed
1 onion, chopped
2 ribs celery, sliced
1 tablespoon oil
1 tablespoon chili powder
1 (15 ounce) can stewed tomatoes
2 (14 ounce) cans beef broth
½ (8 ounce) package egg noodles
1 green bell pepper, seeded, chopped

- Cook and stir cubed steak, onion and celery in soup pot with oil for 15 minutes or until beef browns.

- Stir in 2 cups water, 1 teaspoon salt, chili powder, stewed tomatoes and beef broth.

- Bring to boil, reduce heat and simmer for 1 hour 30 minutes to 2 hours or until beef is tender.

- Stir in noodles and bell pepper and heat to boiling. Reduce heat and simmer for 10 to 15 minutes or until noodles are tender. Serves 6.

Meatball Supper

1 (18 ounce) package frozen, cooked Italian meatballs
2 (14 ounce) cans beef broth
2 (15 ounce) cans Italian stewed tomatoes
1 (16 ounce) package frozen stew vegetables

- Place meatballs, beef broth and stewed tomatoes in large saucepan. Bring to boil, reduce heat and simmer for 10 minutes or until meatballs are thoroughly hot.

- Add vegetables and cook on medium heat for 10 minutes. Serves 6 to 8.

TIP: If you like your soup thicker, mix 2 tablespoons cornstarch in ¼ cup water and stir into soup, bring to boiling and stir constantly until soup thickens.

In southern Italy, soup is said to relieve your hunger, quench your thirst, fill your stomach, clean your teeth, make you sleep, help you digest and color your cheeks.

No-Brainer Heidelberg Warm-Up

2 (10 ounce) cans potato soup
1 (10 ounce) can cream of celery soup
1 soup can milk
6 slices salami, chopped
10 green onions, chopped

- Cook potato soup, celery soup and milk in large saucepan on medium heat, stirring constantly, just until thoroughly hot.

- Saute salami and onions in sprayed skillet and add to soup.

- Heat thoroughly and serve hot. Serves 6.

You can make a base for any soup by starting with canned soups, broths, prepared soup bases, clam juice, tomato juice and some bacon. Bacon is the secret ingredient that really adds something to canned soups.

Black Bean Barbecue Fix

1 onion, finely chopped
2 tablespoons olive oil
2 teaspoons minced garlic
2 (14 ounce) cans chicken broth
3 (15 ounce) cans black beans, rinsed, drained
1 (10 ounce) can diced tomatoes and
     green chilies
1 pound shredded barbecue beef
2 tablespoons red wine vinegar
Shredded Monterey Jack cheese

- Saute onion in oil in soup pot over medium heat, stir in garlic and saute 1 more minute.

- Stir in broth, beans and tomatoes and green chilies. Reduce heat, simmer for 15 minutes and stir often.

- Process 1 cup bean mixture in food processor until smooth. Return puree to soup pot, add beef and simmer for 10 minutes.

- Stir in vinegar and garnish each bowl with cheese. Serves 6 to 8.

Black Bean-Chile Soup

2 (14 ounce) cans chicken broth
3 (15 ounce) cans black beans, rinsed, drained
2 (10 ounce) cans diced tomatoes and green
chilies
1 onion, chopped
1 teaspoon ground cumin
1 tablespoon minced garlic
2 - 3 cups cooked, finely diced ham

- Combine chicken broth and black beans in sprayed slow cooker and cook on HIGH just long enough for ingredients to get hot. With potato masher, mash about half of beans in cooker.

- Reduce heat to LOW and add tomatoes and green chilies, onion, cumin, garlic, ham and ¾ cup water.

- Cover and cook for 5 to 6 hours. Serves 6.

Which hand should you use to stir soup?

Neither. Use a spoon, dummy.

Sailor's Slow-Cook Navy Beans

Better than Grandma's!

1½ cups dried navy beans
1 bell pepper, seeded, chopped
1 carrot, finely chopped
2 celery ribs, finely chopped
1 small onion, finely chopped
1 (1 pound) ham hock

- Soak beans for 8 to 12 hours and drain.
  Place all ingredients in sprayed 2-quart slow
  cooker, add 5 cups water, ½ teaspoon salt
  and a little pepper. Cook for 8 to 10 hours
  on LOW.

- Remove ham hock and discard skin, fat and
  bone. Cut meat in small pieces and place in
  soup. Beans can be mashed, if desired.
  Serves 4 to 6.

Add a pinch of red pepper flakes to your favorite soup for a flavorful addition.

Cabbage-Ham Starter

1 (16 ounce) package cabbage slaw
1 onion, chopped
1 teaspoon minced garlic
2 (14 ounce) cans chicken broth
1 (15 ounce) can stewed tomatoes
2 cups cooked, cubed ham
¼ cup packed brown sugar
2 tablespoons lemon juice

- Combine cabbage, onion, garlic, chicken broth and 1 cup water in large, heavy soup pot. Bring to boil, reduce heat and simmer for 20 minutes.

- Stir in tomatoes, ham, 1 teaspoon salt, brown sugar, lemon juice and a little pepper. Heat just until soup is thoroughly hot. Serves 6.

The ladies of the French court of Louis XI mostly ate soups and broth because they believed that chewing would cause wrinkles and ruin their facial features.

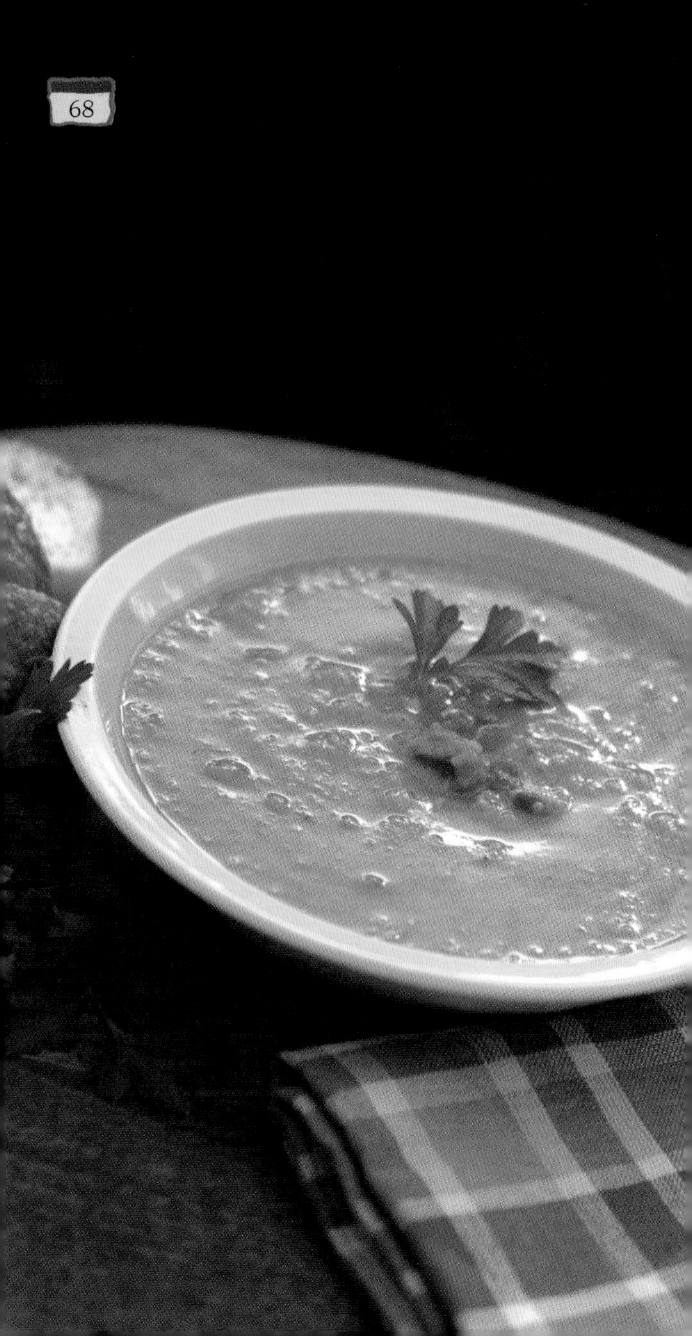

Split Pea and Tortellini Medley

⅓ cup dry split peas
2 tablespoons dried minced onion
1½ teaspoons dried basil
1 tablespoon minced garlic
¾ cup cheese-filled tortellini
1 cup cooked, diced ham
2 (14 ounce) cans chicken broth

- Combine all ingredients with 1½ cups water in soup pot.

- Bring to a boil, reduce heat and simmer for 45 minutes or until peas are tender. Serves 6.

Fresh herbs provide the best flavors. Dried herbs are convenient, affordable and the flavor is more concentrated than fresh herbs. You need to use more twice as many fresh herbs than dried herbs.

Wild Rice-Ham Soup

1 (6 ounce) box long grain-wild rice
1 (16 ounce) package frozen chopped bell
   peppers and onions
1 (10 ounce) can cream of celery soup
2 (14 ounce) cans chicken broth
2 cups cooked, diced ham
2 (15 ounce) cans black-eyed peas and
   jalapenos with liquid

- Cook rice according to package directions.
  Combine rice, bell peppers and onions,
  celery soup, broth, ham, and black-eyed
  peas in soup pot.

- Bring to a boil, reduce heat and simmer
  for 20 minutes. Serves 6.

*Savory soups and stews
often taste better if made
a day or two in advance and
reheated just before serving.*

Miss Bessie's Black-Eyed Pea Supper

1½ cups dry black-eyed peas
2 - 3 cups cooked, cubed ham
1 (15 ounce) can whole kernel corn, drained
1 (10 ounce) package frozen cut okra, thawed
1 onion, chopped
1 large potato, peeled, cubed
2 teaspoons Cajun seasoning
2 (14 ounce) can chicken broth
2 (15 ounce) cans Mexican stewed tomatoes

- Rinse peas and drain. Combine peas and 5 cups water in large saucepan. Bring to boil, reduce heat and simmer for about 10 minutes. Drain peas and pour into sprayed 5 to 6-quart slow cooker.

- Add ham, corn, okra, onion, potato, seasoning, broth and 2 cups water into slow cooker, cover and cook on LOW for 6 to 8 hours.

- Add stewed tomatoes and continue cooking for additional 1 hour. Serves 6.

Tomato and White Bean Soup

2 tablespoons olive oil
1 onion, chopped
1 green bell pepper, seeded, chopped
1 (15 ounce) can diced tomatoes
2 (14 ounce) cans chicken broth
2 (15 ounce) cans navy beans, rinsed, drained
1½ cups cooked, cubed ham
½ cup chopped fresh parsley

- Combine olive oil, onion, bell pepper in large saucepan and saute for 5 minutes and stir constantly.

- Stir in tomatoes, broth, navy beans and ham and bring to boil. Reduce heat and simmer for 10 minutes.

- Pour into individual soup bowls and sprinkle parsley on top. Serves 4.

If your sauce, soup or stew is too salty, add a peeled potato to the pot and it will absorb the extra salt.

Good Ol' Bean Soup

3 tablespoons olive oil
1 cup shredded carrots
1 (16 ounce) package frozen chopped bell
peppers and onions
2 (14 ounce) cans chicken broth
2 (15 ounce) cans pinto beans with jalapenos
with liquid
2 cups cooked, diced ham

- Combine oil, carrots, and bell peppers and onions in soup pot and cook for 10 minutes.

- Add broth, pinto beans, ham and ½ cup water. Bring to boil, reduce heat and simmer for 15 minutes. Serves 6.

In ancient Greece, soup made of peas, lentils and beans was sold in stalls on the street as perhaps the world's first fast food.

Hearty Bean and Ham Fare

What a great supper for a cold winter night!

1 (15 ounce) can sliced carrots, drained
1 cup chopped celery
¼ cup (½ stick) butter
2 - 3 cups cooked, diced ham
2 (15 ounce) cans navy beans with liquid
2 (15 ounce) cans jalapeno pinto beans
     with liquid
2 (14 ounce) cans chicken broth
2 teaspoons chili powder

- Cook carrots and celery in soup pot with butter for about 8 minutes until tender-crisp.

- Add diced ham, navy beans, pinto beans, chicken broth, chili powder and a little salt and pepper. Bring to boil and stir constantly for 3 minutes. Reduce heat and simmer for 15 minutes. Serves 8.

TIP: Cornbread is great with this soup.

" When do 24-hour cafes start serving the soup of the day?" Steve Riches

Ham and Black Bean Soup

2 cups dried black beans
1 cup cooked, diced ham
1 onion, chopped
1 carrot, chopped
2 (14 ounce) cans chicken broth
1 tablespoon ground cumin
2 tablespoons fresh cilantro
1 tablespoon chili powder

- Wash beans, soak overnight and drain. Except for sour cream, place all ingredients and 1 teaspoon salt with 10 cups water in large, heavy soup pot. Bring to boil, reduce heat and simmer for 3 hours or until beans are tender.

- Add more water or chicken broth if needed. Make sure there is enough water in pot to make soup consistency and not too thick.

- Place few cups at a time in food processor (using steel blade) or blender and puree until smooth. Add sour cream and reheat soup. Serve in individual bowls. Serves 8.

Ham Bone, Ham Bone

1 ham bone
1 (10 ounce) package frozen butter beans or
  lima beans
1½ pounds cooked, cubed ham or chicken
1 (15 ounce) can stewed tomatoes
3 cups small, whole okra
2 large onions, diced
Rice, cooked

- Boil ham hock in 1½ quarts water for about
  1 hour 30 minutes in soup pot.

- Add remaining ingredients with a little salt
  and pepper and simmer for additional 1 hour.
  Remove ham hock and serve over rice. Serves 6.

" Hambone, Hambone
Trying to eat
Ketchup on his elbow, pickle
    on his feet
Bread in the basket
Chicken in the stew
Supper on the fire for me
    and you."

- Hambone (Red Saunders/Leon
    Washington) Bill Haley

Apache Pork and Hominy Soup

2 pounds pork shoulder, cubed
1 onion, chopped
2 ribs celery, sliced
2 (15 ounce) cans yellow hominy with liquid
2 (15 ounce) cans stewed tomatoes
2 (14 ounce) cans chicken broth
1 tablespoon ground cumin
Tortillas
Shredded cheese
Green onions, chopped

- Sprinkle pork cubes with a little salt and pepper and brown in skillet. Place in sprayed 5 to 6-quart slow cooker.

- Combine onion, celery, hominy, stewed tomatoes, broth, cumin and 1 cup water and pour over pork. Cover and cook on HIGH for 6 to 7 hours.

- Serve with warmed, buttered tortillas and top each bowl of soup with some shredded cheese and green onions. Serves 6.

Sausage-Tortellini Soup

1 pound Italian sausage
1 onion, chopped
2 (14 ounce) cans beef broth
1 medium zucchini, halved, sliced
1 (15 ounce) can Italian stewed tomatoes
1 (9 ounce) package refrigerated meat-filled
    tortellini
Mozzarella cheese

- Cook and stir sausage and onion in soup pot on medium heat until sausage is light brown.

- Drain and stir in beef broth, 1½ cups water, zucchini, tomatoes, tortellini and a little salt and pepper.

- Bring to a boil, reduce heat and simmer for 20 minutes or until tortellini are tender.

- Ladle into individual soup bowls and sprinkle each serving with cheese. Serves 6.

To soak up the extra fat in soups, float a large leaf of lettuce on the top. Ice cubes do the same thing.

Bonzo Garbanzo Soup

**1 (16 ounce) package frozen chopped bell
    peppers and onions**
Olive oil
1 pound Italian sausage, cut up
1 (14 ounce) can beef broth
1 (15 ounce) can Italian stewed tomatoes
**2 (15 ounce) cans garbanzo beans, rinsed,
    drained**

- Saute bell peppers and onions in soup pot with
  a little oil. Add Italian sausage and cook until
  brown. Stir in beef broth, stewed tomatoes and
  garbanzo beans.

- Bring mixture to boil, reduce heat and simmer
  for about 30 minutes. Serves 6.

One quart of soup served
as a side dish will be enough
for one serving for six people.
For a main course, one quart
will serve three people with
two servings each.

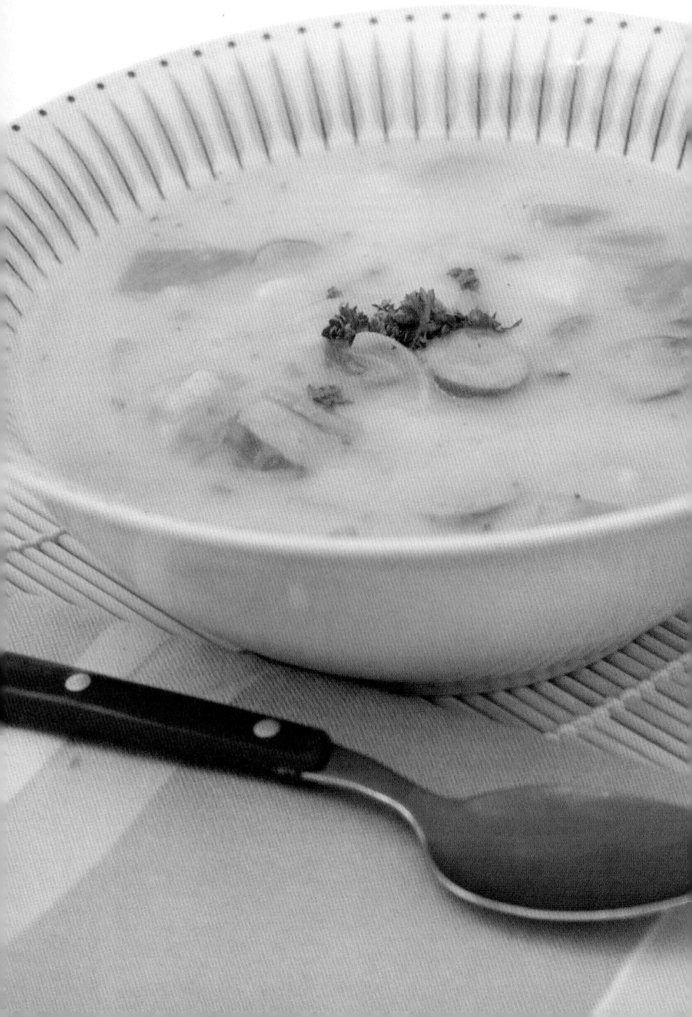

Potato-Sausage Feast

1 pound pork sausage links
1 cup chopped celery
1 cup chopped onion
2 (10 ounce) cans potato soup
1 (14 ounce) can chicken broth

- Cut sausage into 1-inch diagonal slices. Brown in large heavy soup pot, drain and place in separate bowl.

- Leave about 2 tablespoons sausage drippings in skillet and saute celery and onion.

- Add potato soup, ¾ cup water, chicken broth and sausage. Bring to boil, reduce heat and simmer for 20 minutes. Serves 4.

TIP: Add 1 cup sliced carrots for more color.

To thicken a broth for a quick-and-easy soup, puree frozen vegetables and add to broth. This will be your base for other ingredients.

Loaded Baked Potato Soup

5 large baking potatoes
¾ cup (1½ sticks) butter
⅔ cup flour
6 cups milk
**1 (8 ounce) package shredded cheddar cheese,
   divided**
1 (3 ounce) package real bacon bits
1 bunch fresh green onions, chopped, divided
1 (8 ounce) carton sour cream

- Cook potatoes in microwave or bake for 1 hour
  at 400°. Cut potatoes in half lengthwise, scoop
  out flesh and save. Discard potato shells.

- Melt butter in large soup pot over low heat, add
  flour and stir until smooth. Gradually add milk
  and cook over medium heat, stirring constantly,
  until mixture thickens.

- Stir in potatoes, half cheese, bacon bits,
  2 tablespoons green onions and a little salt
  and pepper. Cook until hot, but do not boil.

- Stir in sour cream and cook just until hot.
  Spoon into soup bowls and sprinkle remaining
  cheese and green onions over each serving.
  Serves 6.

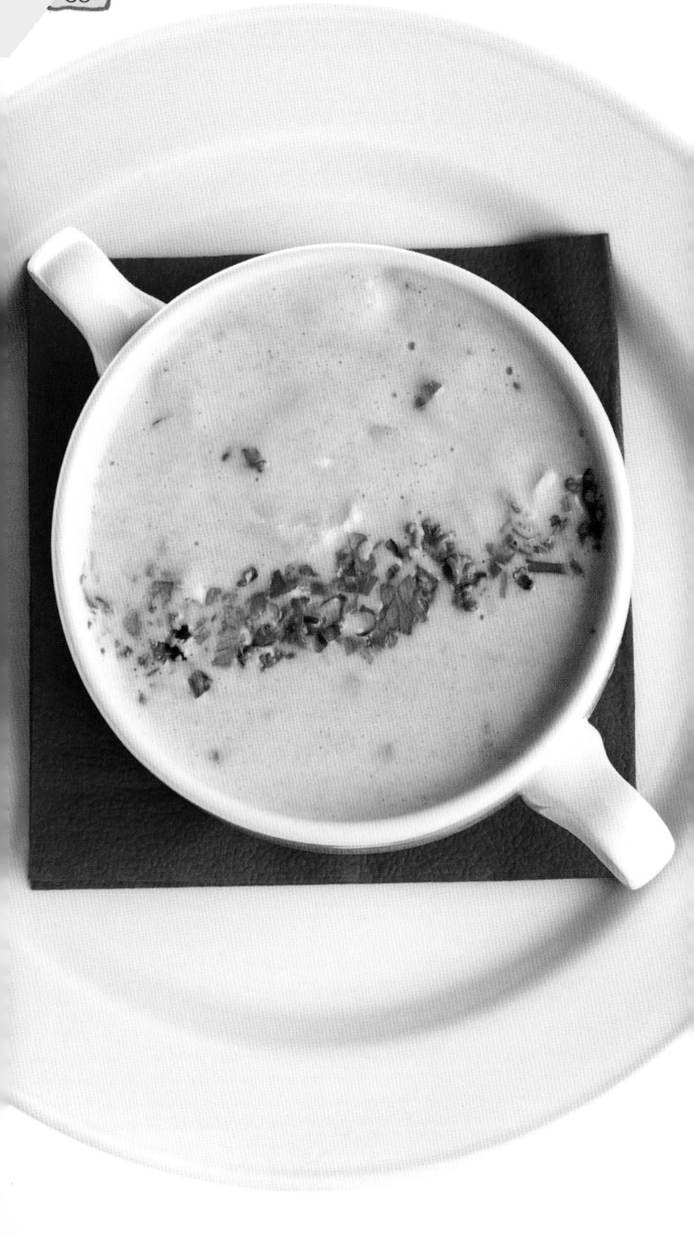

Spiked Crab Net

1 (1 ounce) packet onion soup mix
1 (6 ounce) can crabmeat with liquid, flaked
1 (8 ounce) carton whipping cream
½ cup white wine

- Dissolve soup mix with 2 cups water in saucepan.

- Add crabmeat, crab liquid and whipping cream. Season with a little salt and pepper.

- Heat, but do not boil, and simmer for 20 minutes.

- Stir in wine, heat and serve warm.   Serves 4.

Wine is a great flavor addition to soups and stews. When using wine or alcohol in soup, use less salt because the wine tends to intensify saltiness. About ¼ cup wine should be used for each quart of soup.

Fresh Oyster Boat

2 (14 ounce) cans chicken broth
1 large onion, chopped
3 ribs celery, sliced
2 teaspoons minced garlic
2 (1 pint) cartons fresh oysters, rinsed, drained
½ cup (1 stick) butter
¼ cup flour
2 cups milk
1 tablespoon dried parsley

- Combine broth, onion, celery and garlic in soup pot. Bring to boil, reduce heat and simmer, stirring occasionally for 30 minutes.

- Boil oysters in 2 cups water in saucepan for 2 minutes, stirring often or until edges of oysters begin to curl.

- Remove oysters with slotted spoon, coarsely chop half and set aside. Pour oyster stock into soup pot with vegetables.

- Melt butter in saucepan over medium heat, gradually whisk in flour and cook for 1 minute. Add flour mixture to soup pot and simmer, stirring occasionally over medium heat for 3 minutes.

- Stir in chopped oysters, milk, parsley and a little salt and pepper. Cook and stir occasionally over medium heat for 8 minutes or until mixture thickens. Stir in remaining whole oysters. Serves 6 to 8.

Homestyle Seafood Bisque

¼ cup (½ stick) butter
1 (8 ounce) package frozen salad shrimp, thawed
1 (6 ounce) can crab, drained, flaked
1 (15 ounce) can whole new potatoes, drained, sliced
1 teaspoon minced garlic
½ cup flour
2 (14 ounce) cans chicken broth, divided
1 cup half-and-half cream

- Melt butter in large saucepan on medium heat. Add shrimp, crab, new potatoes and garlic and cook for 10 minutes.

- Stir in flour and cook, stirring constantly for 3 minutes. Gradually add chicken broth, cook and stir until mixture thickens.

- Stir in half-and-half cream and a little salt and pepper, stirring constantly and cook just until mixture is thoroughly hot; do not boil. Serves 6.

Warm-Your-Soul Soup

3 (14 ounce) cans chicken broth
1 (15 ounce) can Italian-stewed tomatoes
      with liquid
½ cup chopped onion
¾ cup chopped celery
1 carrot, sliced
½ (12 ounce) box fettuccini

- Combine chicken broth, tomatoes, onion, celery and carrot in large soup pot. Bring to a boil and simmer until onion, celery and carrot are almost done.

- Add fettuccini and cook according to package directions. Season with a little salt and pepper. Serves 6.

> Pasta has been a very popular food from its beginning, but it was not served on the tables of the rich and famous because it was eaten with the hands. Then a member of the Spanish court of King Ferdinand II invented the fork in the 1400's especially for eating pasta and history was made.

Homemade Tomato Soup

3 (15 ounce) cans whole tomatoes with liquid
1 (14 ounce) can chicken broth
1 tablespoon sugar
1 tablespoon minced garlic
1 tablespoon balsamic vinegar
¾ cup whipping cream

- Puree tomatoes in batches with blender and pour into large saucepan. Add chicken broth, sugar, garlic, balsamic vinegar and a little salt.

- Bring to a boil, reduce heat and simmer for 15 minutes.

- Pour in whipping cream, stir constantly and heat until soup is thoroughly hot. Serves 4.

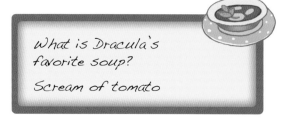

What is Dracula's favorite soup?

Scream of tomato

Corn Soup Olé

2 (15 ounce) cans whole kernel corn
½ onion, chopped
2 tablespoons butter
2 tablespoons flour
2 (14 ounce) cans chicken broth
1½ cups half-and-half cream
1 (8 ounce) package shredded cheddar cheese
1 (4 ounce) can diced green chilies

- Saute corn and onion in butter in soup pot. Add flour, ½ teaspoon salt and ¼ teaspoon pepper and cook for 1 minute. Gradually add broth and half-and-half cream while on medium-low heat. Cook and stir until it thickens slightly.

- Add cheddar cheese and green chilies. Heat but do not boil. Serves 6.

TIP: Garnish with tortilla chips and bacon bits.

According to an old Spanish proverb, " Of soup and love, soup is better."

Cream of Mushroom

3 (8 ounce) packages fresh mushrooms
1 small onion, finely chopped
¼ cup (½ stick) butter, melted
½ cup flour
2 (14 ounce) cans chicken broth
1 (1 pint) carton half-and-half cream
1 (8 ounce) carton whipping cream
¼ cup dry white wine
1 teaspoon dried tarragon

- Coarsely chop and saute mushrooms and onion in butter in large soup pot. Add flour and stir until smooth.

- Add broth, half-and-half cream, whipping cream, wine, tarragon and about 1 teaspoon salt and stir constantly.

- Bring to boil, reduce heat to medium and cook for 20 minutes or until mixture thickens. Stir often. Serves 6.

Customer: Waiter, what's this fly doing in my soup?

Waiter: Looks like the breaststroke to me, sir.

Cream of Carrot

1 small onion, chopped
2 tablespoons butter
6 carrots, chopped
2 tablespoons dry white wine
2 (14 ounce) cans chicken broth
1 teaspoon ground nutmeg
1 (8 ounce) carton whipping cream, whipped

- Saute onion in butter and add carrots, wine, chicken broth, nutmeg, ½ teaspoon pepper and a little salt in large saucepan.

- Bring to boil, reduce heat and simmer for 30 minutes or until carrots are tender.

- Pour half of carrot mixture into blender, cover and blend on medium speed until mixture is smooth.

- Repeat with remaining mixture. Return to saucepan and heat just until hot. Stir in cream. Serves 6.

North Americans love soup. Would you believe 99% of all households buy soups.

Cream of Artichoke

2 shallots, finely chopped
2 tablespoons butter
2 tablespoons flour
1 (14 ounce) can chicken broth
**1¼ cups artichoke hearts, rinsed, drained,
    chopped**
3 tablespoons fresh minced parsley, divided
1¼ cups half-and-half cream

- Saute shallots in saucepan with butter until they are transparent. Add flour, stir to remove lumps and cook.

- Remove from heat and stir in chicken broth, artichoke hearts and 2 tablespoons parsley.

- Return to medium heat and cook for 5 minutes. Puree mixture in blender. Strain pureed mixture through coarse sieve and return to clean saucepan.

- Heat on medium, slowly add half-and-half cream and blend thoroughly. Serve hot or cold. Garnish with remaining parsley, if desired. Serves 4.

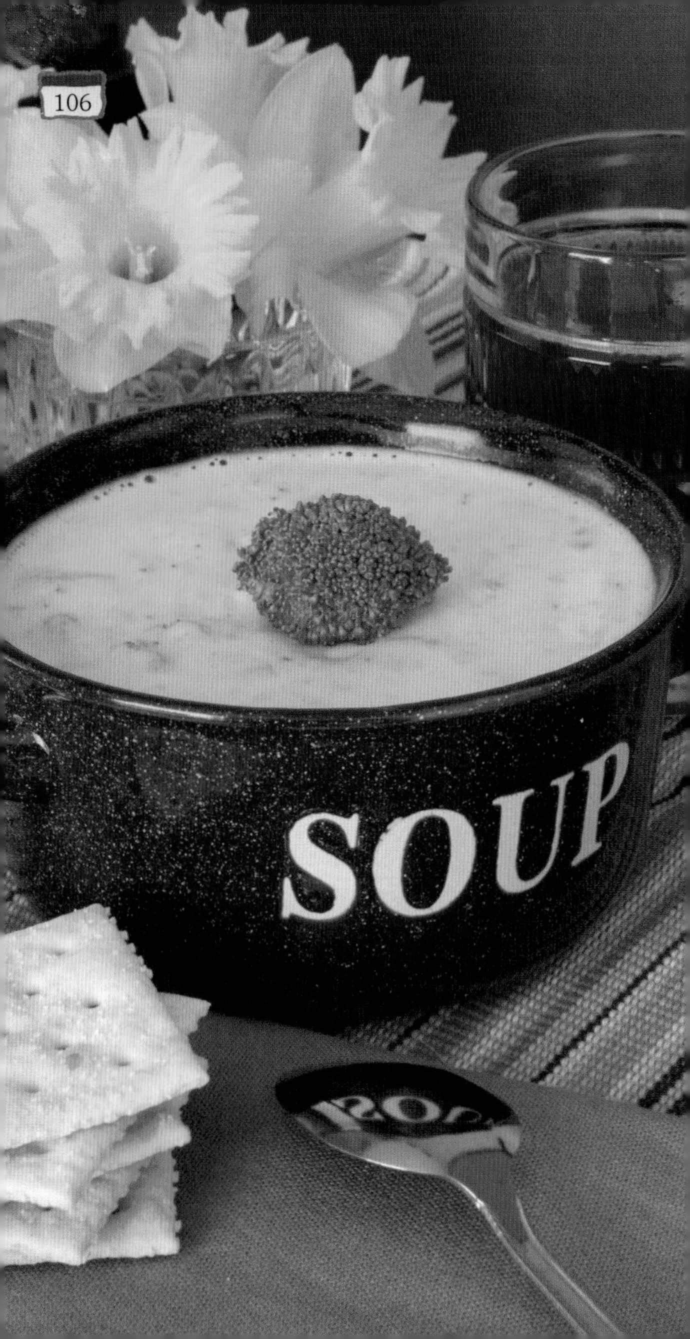
SOUP

Delicious Broccoli-Cheese Soup

1 (16 ounce) package frozen chopped broccoli, thawed
1 (12 ounce) package cubed Velveeta® cheese
1 (1 ounce) packet white sauce mix
1 (1 ounce) packet dry vegetable soup mix
1 (12 ounce) can evaporated milk
1 (14 ounce) can chicken broth

- Combine all ingredients plus 2 cups water in large sprayed slow cooker and stir well.

- Cover and cook on LOW for 6 to 7 hours or on HIGH for 3 hours 30 minutes to 4 hours. Stir 1 hour before serving time. Serves 6.

Some of the greatest artists in history were inspired by soup: Pablo Picasso painted "La Soup;" Vincent Van Gosh painted "Bowls and Bottles;" and James McNeill Whistler painted "Soupe a Trois Sous."

Cheese-Topped Broccoli

3 (14 ounce) cans chicken broth
2 ribs celery, sliced
1 onion, chopped
1 medium baking potato, peeled, chopped
1 (16 ounce) package frozen chopped broccoli
1 (1 pint) carton half-and-half cream
1 (5 ounce) package grated parmesan cheese

- Combine broth, ½ cup water, celery, onion and chopped potato in large, heavy soup pot.

- Bring to boil, reduce heat and simmer for 20 minutes or until vegetables are tender.

- Stir in broccoli and boil, reduce heat and simmer for 15 minutes. Stir in half-and-half cream, ¼ teaspoon pepper and a little salt.

- Heat on medium, stirring constantly until soup is thoroughly hot. Ladle into individual soup bowls and sprinkle with parmesan. Serves 6.

When is rabbit soup not good?"
When there's a hare in it!

Country Cheddar Cheese

¾ cup (1½ sticks) butter, divided
2 ribs celery, chopped
1 small onion, finely chopped
1 carrot, peeled, shredded
1 (14 ounce) can chicken broth
⅔ cup flour
1 quart milk
1 (8 ounce) package shredded sharp
    cheddar cheese

- Melt ¼ cup butter in saucepan and cook celery, onion and carrot until tender; stir often. Stir in broth, bring to boil, reduce heat and cook on low heat for 10 minutes.

- While vegetables cook, heat remaining ½ cup butter in large saucepan, stir in flour and cook, stirring constantly until bubbly.

- Remove from heat and gradually add milk. Cook over medium heat, stirring often, until soup thickens, but do not boil.

- Stir in cheese and heat until cheese melts. Stir in vegetable-broth mixture and heat just until hot. Serves 8.

Fireside Pumpkin Harvest

1 (8 ounce) package fresh mushrooms, sliced
3 tablespoons butter
¼ cup flour
2 (14 ounce) cans vegetable broth
1 (15 ounce) can cooked pumpkin
1 (1 pint) carton half-and-half cream
2 tablespoons honey
2 tablespoons sugar
1 teaspoon ground nutmeg

- Saute mushrooms in butter in large saucepan. Add flour, stir well and gradually add broth. Boil and cook for 2 minutes or until mixture thickens.

- Stir in pumpkin, half-and-half cream, honey, sugar and nutmeg. Stir constantly until soup is thoroughly hot. Serves 6.

TIP: If you have some sour cream, a dollop of sour cream on top of the soup is a very nice garnish.

Fiesta Tortilla Soup con Queso

3 (14 ounce) cans chicken broth
2 (15 ounce) cans stewed tomatoes
4 green onions with tops, chopped
1 (7 ounce) cans diced green chilies
1 clove garlic, minced
8 corn tortillas
2 tablespoons oil
1 (16 ounce) package cubed Mexican
**   Velveeta® cheese**

- Pour chicken broth, tomatoes, onions, green chilies and garlic in large saucepan and heat on medium.

- Cut tortillas into long, narrow strips. Fry tortilla strips with hot oil in skillet for about 10 seconds or until strips are crisp. Remove from skillet and drain.

- Heat soup to boiling, reduce heat to low and stir in cheese. Serve in individual bowls and garnish with tortilla strips. Serves 8.

Choice Tomato-Ravioli

1 (15 ounce) can Italian stewed tomatoes
2 (14 ounce) cans chicken broth
1 (12 ounce) packet refrigerated cheese ravioli
2 small zucchini, sliced
4 fresh green onions, sliced

- Combine tomatoes, chicken broth and
  1 teaspoon pepper in large saucepan. Bring
  to boil, reduce heat and simmer for 5 minutes.

- Add ravioli and zucchini and bring to boil,
  reduce heat and simmer for 8 to 10 minutes
  or until ravioli are tender. Sprinkle a few
  sliced green onions over each individual
  serving. Serve 6.

The Italian word "zuppa"
once described a soup served
over a thick piece of bread.
Throughout history, people
have used bread to thicken
soup and add substance to
broth. Today the term "zuppa"
simply means a thick soup.

Jazzy Cauliflower-Potato Soup

1 cup instant mashed potato flakes
½ cup finely chopped scallions, whites only
1 teaspoon caraway seeds
2 (14 ounce) cans chicken broth
1 (16 ounce) package frozen cauliflower florets
**1 (8 ounce) package shredded cheddar
    cheese, divided**

- Combine 1½ cups boiling water, dry mashed potatoes, scallions, caraway seeds, 1½ teaspoons salt, 1 teaspoon pepper and chicken broth in soup pot. Bring to boil, reduce heat to medium and simmer for 10 minutes.

- Stir in cauliflower florets and cook for about 10 minutes or until cauliflower is tender. Stir in half cheddar cheese and serve in individual soup bowls with couple tablespoons cheese over top of each serving. Serves 8.

Andy Warhol said he painted soup cans because he had soup for lunch every day for 20 years.

French Onion Soup

5 - 6 sweet onions, thinly sliced
1 clove garlic, minced
2 tablespoons butter
2 (14 ounce) cans beef broth
2 teaspoons Worcestershire sauce
6 (1 inch) slices French bread
6 slices Swiss cheese

- Cook onions and garlic on low heat (do not brown) in hot butter in large skillet for about 20 minutes and stir several times.

- Transfer onion mixture to sprayed 4 to 5-quart slow cooker. Add beef broth, Worcestershire sauce and 1 cup water.

- Cover and cook on LOW for 5 to 8 hours or on HIGH for 2 hours 30 minutes to 3 hours.

- Before serving soup, toast bread slices and place cheese slice on top. Broil for 3 to 4 minutes or until cheese is light brown and bubbles. Ladle soup into bowls and top with toast. Serves 6.

Ranchero Black Bean

1 cup dried black beans
3 (14 ounce) cans beef broth
1 large bunch green onions with tops, chopped
3 cloves garlic, minced
½ cup (1 stick) butter
½ cup rice
2 teaspoons cayenne pepper

- Sort beans, rinse and soak in water overnight. Drain beans, transfer to large saucepan and cook for about 2 hours in beef broth.

- Saute onions and garlic in butter in skillet until onions are translucent.

- Transfer onions, garlic, rice, 1 teaspoon salt and cayenne pepper to beans.

- Cook for additional 2 hours or until beans are tender. (Add water if needed.) Serves 6.

TIP: When serving, it is a nice touch to garnish with shredded cheese, sour cream or chopped green onions.

Garbanzo Bean Mix-Up

2 tablespoons olive oil
1 (16 ounce) package frozen chopped bell
 peppers and onions
2 teaspoons minced garlic
1 (15 ounce) can Italian stewed tomatoes
2 (14 ounce) cans vegetable broth
1 (15 ounce) can garbanzo beans, drained
½ cup elbow macaroni
1 (5 ounce) package grated parmesan cheese

- Combine olive oil, bell peppers and onions, and garlic in soup pot and cook, stirring often on medium heat for 5 minutes or until onions are translucent.

- Stir in tomatoes, broth, garbanzo beans and a little salt and pepper and cook for 10 minutes.

- Stir in macaroni and cook for about 15 minutes or until macaroni is al dente (tender, but not overdone). Place about 1 heaping tablespoon parmesan cheese over each serving. Serves 6.

What do you call 2,000 pounds of Chinese soup?

Won Ton

Italian Minestrone

1 (16 ounce) package frozen chopped bell
    peppers and onions
2 teaspoons minced garlic
¼ cup (½ stick) butter
2 (15 ounce) cans Italian stewed tomatoes
2 (14 ounce) cans beef broth
2 (15 ounce) cans kidney beans, drained
2 medium zucchini, cut in half lengthwise, sliced
1 cup elbow macaroni

- Saute bell peppers and onions and garlic in
  butter for about 2 minutes in soup pot. Add
  tomatoes and a little salt and pepper. Bring to
  boil, reduce heat and simmer for 15 minutes,
  stirring occasionally.

- Stir in beef broth, beans, zucchini and macaroni
  and bring to boil. Reduce heat and simmer
  for additional 15 minutes or until macaroni is
  tender. Serves 8.

Minestrone soup comes
from the Italian word
"minestra," which means
minister. Clergy ministered to
the poor by providing bowls of
broth with hearty vegetables.

South-of-the-Border Beef Stew

1½ - 2 pounds boneless, beef chuck roast
1 green bell pepper, seeded
2 onions, coarsely chopped
2 (15 ounce) cans pinto beans with liquid
½ cup rice
1 (14 ounce) can beef broth
2 (15 ounce) cans Mexican stewed tomatoes
1 cup mild or medium green salsa
2 teaspoons ground cumin
Flour tortillas

- Trim beef and cut into 1-inch cubes. Brown beef in large skillet and transfer to sprayed large slow cooker.

- Cut bell pepper into ½-inch slices. Add remaining ingredients with a little salt and 1½ cups water.

- Cover and cook on LOW for 7 to 8 hours. Serve with warm flour tortillas. Serves 8.

Small portions of leftover soup can be frozen and added to new soups later on.

Blue Ribbon Beef Stew

1 (2½ pound) boneless beef chuck roast, cubed
⅓ cup flour
2 (14 ounce) cans beef broth
1 teaspoon dried thyme
2 teaspoons minced garlic
1 pound new (red) potatoes with peel, sliced
2 large carrots, sliced
3 ribs celery, sliced
2 onions, finely chopped

- Dredge beef in flour and 1 teaspoon salt; set aside leftover flour. Brown half beef in stew pot over medium heat for about 10 minutes and transfer to plate.

- Repeat with remaining beef. Add set aside flour to stew pot and cook, stirring constantly, for 1 minute.

- Stir in beef broth, ½ cup water, thyme and garlic and bring to boil Reduce heat, simmer for 50 minutes and stir occasionally.

- Add potatoes, carrots, celery and onion and cook for 30 minutes. Stir in a little salt and pepper; heat to boiling. Serve hot. Serves 6.

Down Home Meat and Potato Stew

2 pounds beef stew meat
2 (15 ounce) cans new potatoes, drained
1 (15 ounce) can sliced carrots, drained
2 (10 ounce) cans French onion soup

- Season meat with a little salt and pepper and cook with 2 cups water in large pot for 1 hour. Add potatoes, carrots and onion soup and mix well.

- Bring to boil, reduce heat and simmer for 30 minutes. Serves 6.

Soup will feed more people if you add rice, barley or pasta.

Blue Norther Winner

When a cold front moves into the south, it's called a "blue norther". This is a great choice for one of those cold, winter days.

1½ pounds lean ground beef
1 (1 ounce) packet taco seasoning
1 (.04 ounce) packet ranch dressing mix
1 (15 ounce) can whole kernel corn, drained
1 (15 ounce) can kidney beans with liquid
2 (15 ounce) cans pinto beans
2 (15 ounce) cans Mexican stewed tomatoes
1 (10 ounce) can diced tomatoes and
  green chilies

- Brown ground beef in large roasting pan. Add both packets seasonings and mix well.

- Add corn, beans, stewed tomatoes, tomatoes and green chilies, and 1 cup water; mix well and simmer for about 30 minutes. Serves 8.

Many soups are better the second day. The flavors of the food and seasonings have a chance to blend.

Stroganoff Stew

1 (1 ounce) packet onion soup mix
2 (10 ounce) cans golden mushroom soup
2 pounds stew meat
1 (8 ounce) carton sour cream
Noodles, cooked

- Preheat oven to 275°.

- Combine soup mix, mushroom soup and
  2 soup cans water and pour over stew meat
  in roasting pan.

- Cover tightly and bake for 6 to 8 hours.

- When ready to serve, stir in sour cream, return
  mixture to oven until it heats thoroughly and
  serve over noodles. Serves 6.

*If you need to add water
to stew, use tap water and
not boiling water because it
may toughen meat.*

Fast Comfort Stew

1½ pounds premium stew meat
2 (10 ounce) cans French onion soup
1 (10 ounce) can cream of onion soup
1 (10 ounce) can cream of celery soup
1 (16 ounce) package frozen stew
    vegetables, thawed

- Place stew meat in sprayed slow cooker. Combine all soups and mix well. Spread evenly over meat, but do not stir.

- Turn slow cooker to HIGH and cook just long enough for ingredients to get hot, about 15 minutes.

- Change heat setting to LOW, cover and cook for 7 hours. Add vegetables and cook for additional 1 hour. Serves 6 to 8.

Customer: "Waiter, I can't find any chicken in this chicken soup?"

Waiter: "Well, you won't find any horse in the horseradish either, sir."

Chucky Clucky Tortellini Stew

1 (9 ounce) package cheese tortellini
2 small yellow squash, halved, sliced
1 onion, chopped
2 (14 ounce) cans chicken broth
1 teaspoon dried rosemary
2 cups cooked, chopped chicken

- Place tortellini, squash and onion in sprayed slow cooker. Stir in broth, rosemary and chicken.

- Cover and cook on LOW for 2 to 4 hours or until tortellini and vegetables are tender. Serves 6 to 8.

The French consider French cuisine to be superior to all other cuisines in the world. Their comment on British cooking is "If it's cold, it's soup; if it's warm, it's beer."

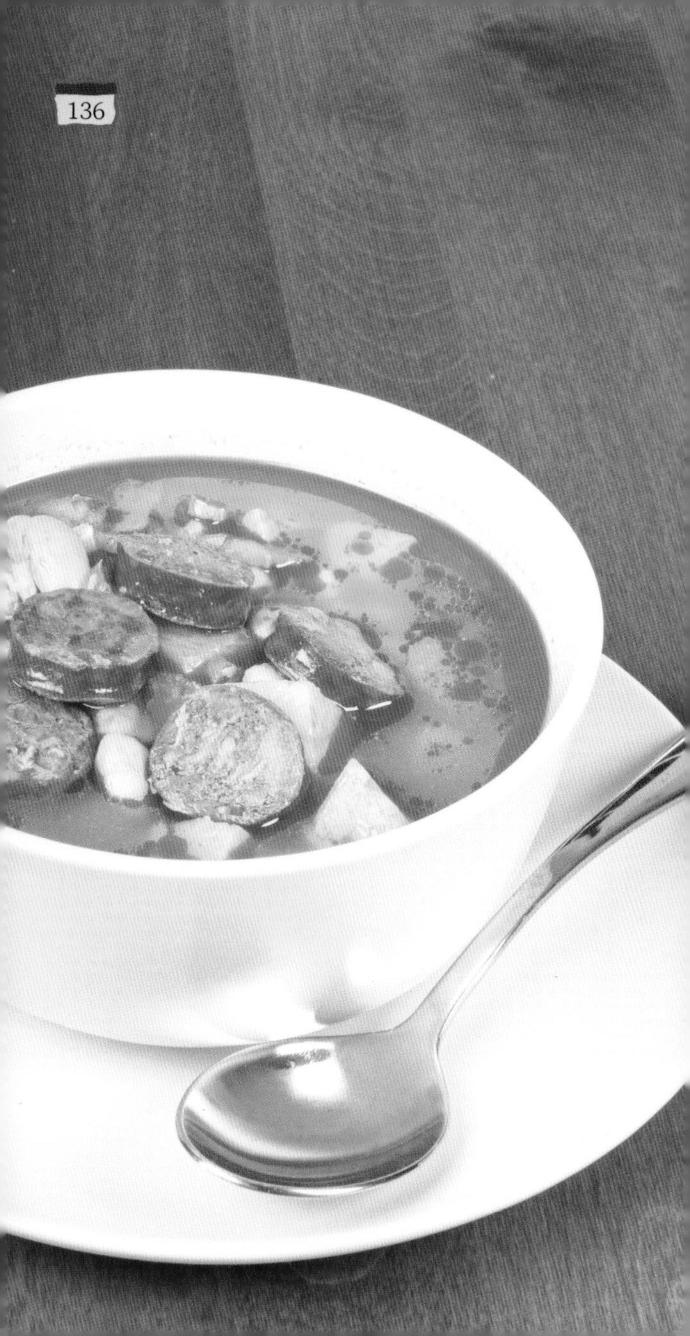

Chicken-Sausage Stew

1 (16 ounce) package frozen stew vegetables
2 (12 ounce) cans chicken breast with liquid
½ pound hot Italian sausage, sliced
2 (15 ounce) cans Italian stewed tomatoes
1 (14 ounce) can chicken broth
1 cup cooked instant rice

- Combine all ingredients except rice and add a little salt in large heavy soup pot. Bring to boil, reduce heat and simmer for 25 minutes.

- Stir in cooked rice during last 5 minutes of cooking time. Serves 8.

Many countries serve soup for breakfast. Breakfast in Japan starts with miso soup, fish broth with rice. Breakfast in France often starts with leftover soup.

Black Bean Stew Supper

1 pound pork sausage link, thinly sliced
2 onions, chopped
3 ribs celery, sliced
Olive oil
3 (15 ounce) cans black beans, drained, rinsed
2 (10 ounce) cans diced tomatoes and
green chilies
2 (14 ounce) cans chicken broth

- Place sausage slices, onion and celery in stew pot with a little oil, cook until sausage is light brown and onion is soft and drain. Add beans, tomatoes and green chilies and broth.

- Bring to boil, reduce heat and simmer for 30 minutes. Take out about 2 cups stew mixture, pour into food processor and pulse until almost smooth.

- Return mixture to pot and stir to thicken stew. Return heat to high until stew is thoroughly hot. Serves 6.

Soups will have a fresh flavor if you add a little chopped parsley or fresh herbs just before serving.

Polish-Vegetable Stew

Olive oil
1 onion, sliced
2 carrots, peeled, sliced
2 (15 ounce) cans stewed tomatoes
2 (15 ounce) cans new potatoes, drained,
    quartered
1 pound Polish sausage, sliced
1 (9 ounce) package coleslaw mix

- Place a little oil in large stew pot. Cook onion and carrots for 3 minutes or until tender-crisp. Add tomatoes and ½ cup water; stir well.

- Stir potatoes and sausage in soup mixture. Bring to boil, reduce heat and simmer for 10 minutes.

- Stir in coleslaw mix and cook on medium heat for additional 8 minutes, stirring occasionally. Serves 6.

It's good idea to refrigerate stews and soups with meat before serving. The fat will rise to the surface and is easy to remove. Just reheat and serve.

Farmhouse Vegetable-Roast Special

3 cups roast beef, cooked, cubed
2 (15 ounce) cans stewed tomatoes
1 (16 ounce) package frozen mixed
vegetables, thawed
2 (14 ounce) cans beef broth

- Combine all ingredients in sprayed 6-quart slow cooker with a little salt and pepper. Cover and cook on LOW for 5 to 7 hours. Serves 6.

TIP: *If you want some crunchy vegetables in your soup, add 1 cup cauliflower florets and 1 cup broccoli florets the last hour of cooking time.*

" I am only one, but I am one. I cannot do everything, but I can do something. And because I cannot do everything, I will not refuse to do the something that I can do. What I can do, I should do. And what I should do, by the grace of God, I will do."
Edward Everett Hale

Pecos Pork Pot

2 pounds boneless pork shoulder, cubed
Olive oil
1 (16 ounce) package frozen chopped bell
peppers and onions
2 cloves garlic, minced
½ cup fresh chopped cilantro
3 tablespoons chili powder
2 (14 ounce) cans chicken broth
2 cups peeled, cubed potatoes
1 (16 ounce) package frozen whole kernel corn
Cornbread

- Brown meat in a little oil in large roasting pan. Stir in bell peppers and onions, garlic, cilantro, chili powder, 1 teaspoon salt, and chicken broth.

- Cover and cook on medium heat for about 45 minutes or until pork is tender.

- Add potatoes and corn. Bring to a boil, turn heat down to medium and cook for additional 30 minutes. Serve with cornbread. Serves 6.

Southwest Pork Stew

2 tablespoons olive oil
2 onions, chopped
1 green bell pepper, seeded, chopped
1 tablespoon minced garlic
2 pounds pork tenderloin, cubed
2 (14 ounce) cans chicken broth
2 baking potatoes, peeled, cubed
2 (15 ounce) cans Mexican stewed tomatoes
2 teaspoons chili powder
1 teaspoon ground cumin
1 tablespoon lime juice

- Place oil in stew pot and saute onion, bell pepper and garlic for 5 minutes.

- Add cubed pork and chicken broth and bring to boil Reduce heat and simmer for 25 minutes.

- Add potatoes and cook for additional 15 minutes or until potatoes are tender.

- Stir in tomatoes, chili powder, cumin, lime juice and a little salt. Heat just until stew is thoroughly hot. Serves 6.

Hearty Chicken-Rice Stew

**2 (12 ounce) cans white chicken meat
with liquid
2 (14 ounce) cans chicken broth
1 (15 ounce) can Mexican stewed tomatoes
2 cups instant brown rice
1 (15 ounce) can whole kernel corn
1 (15 ounce) can cut green beans
1 teaspoon chili powder**

- Combine chicken, broth, stewed tomatoes and rice in heavy soup pot. Bring to boil, reduce heat and simmer for 10 minutes.

- Stir in corn, green beans, chili powder and a little salt and pepper. Bring to boil, reduce heat and cook for 5 minutes. Serves 6 to 8.

Chowders contain any of several varieties of seafood and vegetables. New England-style chowder is made with milk or cream and Manhattan-style chowder is made with tomatoes.

Anytime Chicken-Broccoli Chowder

2 (14 ounce) cans chicken broth
1 (10 ounce) package frozen chopped broccoli
1½ cups dry mashed potato flakes
2½ cups cooked, cut-up chicken breasts
1 (8 ounce) package shredded mozzarella cheese
1 (8 ounce) carton whipping cream
1 cup milk

- Combine broth and broccoli in large saucepan. Bring to boil, reduce heat, cover and simmer for 5 minutes.

- Stir in dry potato flakes and mix until they blend well. Add chicken, cheese, cream, milk, 1 cup water and a little salt and pepper.

- Heat over medium heat and stir occasionally until hot and cheese melts, for about 5 minutes. Serves 8.

TIP: Garnish with chopped green onions.

Whipped Chicken Chowder

3 cups cooked, cubed chicken
1 (14 ounce) can chicken broth
2 (10 ounce) cans cream of potato soup
1 large onion, chopped
3 ribs celery, sliced diagonally
1 (16 ounce) package frozen whole kernel
    corn, thawed
⅔ cup whipping cream

- Combine all ingredients except cream in large soup pot with ¾ cup water.

- Cover and cook on low heat for about 45 minutes. Add whipping cream and heat for additional 10 minutes on low. Do not boil. Serves 6.

Clam Chowder Snap

1 (10 ounce) can New England clam chowder
1 (10 ounce) can cream of celery soup
1 (10 ounce) can cream of potato soup
1 (6.5 ounce) can chopped clams, drained
1 soup can milk

- Combine all ingredients in saucepan. Heat and stir. Serves 4.

Cauliflower-Crab Chowder

1 (16 ounce) package frozen cauliflower
¼ cup (½ stick) butter
¼ cup flour
1 (14 ounce) can chicken broth
1½ cups milk
1 (3 ounce) package cream cheese, cubed
1 (2 ounce) jar chopped pimento, drained
1 (8 ounce) package refrigerated, imitation crabmeat, drained

- Cook cauliflower in ¾ cup water in large saucepan until tender-crisp.

- In separate saucepan, melt butter, stir in flour and mix well. Add broth, milk and cream cheese and cook, stirring constantly, until thick and bubbly.

- Add mixture to saucepan with cauliflower and stir in pimento and a little salt and pepper.

- Stir in crab and heat just until thoroughly hot. Serves 4.

Harbor Cod-Corn

8 slices bacon
1 pound cod, cut into bite-size pieces
2 large baking potatoes, thinly sliced
3 ribs celery, sliced
1 onion, chopped
1 (15 ounce) can whole kernel corn
1 (8 ounce) carton whipping cream

- Fry bacon in large, heavy soup pot, remove bacon and drain. Crumble bacon and set aside.

- Drain fat from soup pot and stir in 2½ cups water, cod, potatoes, celery, onion, corn and a little salt and pepper. Bring to boil, reduce heat, cover and simmer for about 20 minutes or until fish and potatoes are done.

- Stir in cream and heat just until chowder is thoroughly hot. When serving, sprinkle crumbled bacon over each serving. Serves 6.

The word chowder comes from the French word "chaudiere," a caldron in which fishermen made their stews fresh from the sea.

'Who Dat' Seafood Gumbo

¼ cup (½ stick) butter
¼ cup flour
1½ - 2 pounds fresh okra, sliced
2 (15 ounce) cans whole tomatoes, chopped
½ cup minced onion
1 pound shrimp, peeled, cleaned
1 pound crabmeat, flaked, drained
1 (1 pint) carton fresh oysters with liquor
Rice, cooked

- Melt butter in heavy skillet and add flour. Stir well over medium heat to make smooth, paste-like roux.

- When roux is rich brown color, add a little salt and pepper and mix well. Add 2 quarts water, okra, tomatoes and onion. Cook on low for 20 minutes.

- Add all seafood and cook on medium-low for 30 minutes or until desired consistency. Serve over rice. Serves 8.

TIP: Garnish with sliced green onions.

Cheesy Chicken Chili

1 (28 ounce) can diced tomatoes
1 (15 ounce) can kidney beans, rinsed, drained
1 (15 ounce) can pinto beans, drained
2 (14 ounce) cans chicken broth
2 (12 ounce) cans chicken breasts with liquid
1 tablespoon chili powder
1 (8 ounce) package shredded Mexican 4-cheese
   blend, divided

- Combine tomatoes, kidney beans, pinto beans, broth, chicken, chili powder and a little salt and pepper in soup pot.

- Bring to boil, reduce heat and simmer for 25 minutes.

- Stir in half cheese and spoon into individual soup bowls. Sprinkle remaining cheese on top of each serving. Serves 8.

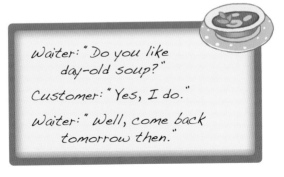

Waiter: "Do you like day-old soup?"

Customer: "Yes, I do."

Waiter: "Well, come back tomorrow then."

Deer Camp Venison Chili

2 onions, chopped
2½ pounds ground venison
1 (15 ounce) can Mexican stewed tomatoes
½ (15 ounce) can beef broth
¾ cup red wine
2 teaspoons minced garlic
3 tablespoons chili powder
1 teaspoon ground cumin

- Cook onions over medium-high heat until translucent. Add venison and brown until meat crumbles; stir often.

- Stir in beef broth, tomatoes, wine, garlic, chili powder, cumin and a little salt. Bring to boil, reduce heat and simmer for 1 hour, stirring occasionally. Remove salt pork before serving. Serves 6.

Herbs will have a more intense flavor if they are added when the soup is almost ready to serve.

Quick Vegetarian Chili

2 (15 ounce) cans stewed tomatoes
1 (15 ounce) can kidney beans, rinsed, drained
1 (15 ounce) can pinto beans with liquid
1 onion, chopped
1 green bell pepper, seeded, chopped
1 tablespoon chili powder
1 (12 ounce) package elbow macaroni
¼ cup (½ stick) butter, sliced

- Combine tomatoes, kidney beans, pinto beans, onion, bell pepper, chili powder and 1 cup water in soup pot. Cover and cook on medium heat for 1 hour.

- Cook macaroni according to package directions, drain and add butter. Stir until butter melts. Add macaroni to chili and mix well. Serves 6.

If you cook pasta before adding it to soup, you eliminate all the starch from the pasta. If cooked, add pasta just before serving. Leftover pasta works well too.

White Lightning Chili

1½ cups dried navy beans
3 (14 ounce) cans chicken broth
2 tablespoons butter
1 onion, chopped
3 cups cooked, chopped chicken
1½ teaspoons ground cumin
1 teaspoon cayenne pepper

- Sort and wash beans, cover with water and soak overnight. Drain beans and place in soup pot and add broth, butter, 1 cup water and onion.

- Bring to boil, reduce heat and cover. Simmer for 2 hours and stir occasionally.

- With potato masher, mash half of beans in soup pot. Add chicken, cumin and cayenne pepper. Bring to a boil, reduce heat and cover. Simmer for additional 30 minutes. Serves 6 to 8.

TIP: Line serving bowls with flour tortillas. Spoon in chili and top with shredded Monterey Jack cheese.

Cadillac Chili

2 pounds chili ground beef
1 onion, chopped
Olive oil
1 (15 ounce) can tomato sauce
1 (10 ounce) can diced tomatoes and
green chilies
4 tablespoons ground cumin
2 tablespoons chili powder
1 (15 ounce) can pinto beans with liquid

- Combine meat and onion in a little oil in large roasting pan and brown. Add tomato sauce, tomatoes and green chilies, cumin, chili powder, 1 cup water and a little salt.

- Bring to a boil, reduce heat and simmer for 2 hours. Add beans and heat until thoroughly hot. Serves 6.

You can thicken soups
by adding quick-cooking oats,
a grated potato or mashing
some of the vegetables.

Hearty Beef Chili

3 tablespoons olive oil, divided
2 pounds round steak, cubed
2 onions, chopped
4 cloves garlic, minced
¼ cup tomato paste
3 tablespoons chili powder
1 teaspoon ground cumin
2 (15 ounce) cans Mexican stewed tomatoes
    with liquid
1 (10 ounce) can beef broth
1 (15 ounce) can pinto beans, drained

- Heat 1 tablespoon oil in soup pot and brown beef. Transfer meat to bowl and set aside.

- Heat remaining 2 tablespoons oil in soup pot and add onion and garlic. Cook for about 3 minutes, stir in tomato paste, chili powder, 1 teaspoon each of salt and pepper, and cumin.

- Add tomatoes, meat, beef broth and 1 cup water. Bring to boil, reduce heat and simmer for 2 hours or until meat is tender and chili thickens.

- Stir in beans and continue simmering for about 20 minutes. Serves 6.

Turkey-Veggie Chili

1 pound ground turkey
Olive oil
2 (15 ounce) cans pinto beans with liquid
1 (15 ounce) can great northern beans
with liquid
1 (14 ounce) can chicken broth
2 (15 ounce) cans Mexican stewed tomatoes
1 (8 ounce) can whole kernel corn, drained
1 (10 ounce) package frozen chopped bell
peppers and onions, thawed
2 teaspoons minced garlic
2 teaspoons ground cumin

- Cook and brown turkey in skillet with a little oil and place in sprayed large slow cooker. Add beans, broth, tomatoes, corn, bell peppers and onions, garlic, cumin, and a little salt and stir well.

- Cover and cook on LOW for 4 to 5 hours. Serves 8.

TIP: If you want to get "fancy," top each serving with dab of sour cream or 1 tablespoon shredded cheddar cheese.

Who's Who:
Soups, Stews, Chowders and Chilis

Soups

Most of us know or have a pretty good idea of the difference between **soups** and **stews**. Soups are thin and stews are thick. It's very simple. But if you want to know more about these comforting dishes, look deeper to learn many other differences.

Soups start with liquid, usually hot water. Meats, beans and vegetables are simmered to extract the flavors of the ingredients and that is the broth or stock used as the base. As they boil they break down and mix with the liquid for a distinctive blend of flavors.

Clear soups are called broth, bouillon or consommé. Purees are mixes of vegetables and liquid thickened by the starch in the vegetables. Other types of purees are thickened with cream, milk, eggs, rice, flour or grains.

Stews

Stews are very similar to **soups** because they are combinations of vegetables and meats cooked in a broth or stock. They are thickened with most of the same ingredients as **soups**, but there is a distinct

Continued next page...

Continued from previous page...

difference. **Stews** usually have larger pieces of meat and vegetables than do **soups**. These large pieces are simmered for a long time to tenderize the ingredients.

Stews are usually served as a main course and **soups** are usually served as a first course. **Stews** are usually heartier and more filling than **soups**, but there is little difference in the popularity of both.

Chowders

Chowders are similar to stews, but mainly consist of fish or clams, potatoes, and onions. New England clam **chowder** has a cream base and Manhattan clam **chowder** has a tomato base. There is also corn **chowder** with a cream base.

Chilis

Chile with an "e" refers to the many peppers available for cooking. **Chili** with an "i" refers to the state dish of Texas. Dallas' Frank Tolbert, the founder of the International Terlingua Chili Cook-off and chili aficionado, called **chili** "a bowl of red" to reflect the proper color of the dish.

Americans eat more than 10,000,000,000 (billion) bowls of soup each year.

Index

Cookbooks Published by Cookbook Resources, LLC
Bringing Family and Friends to the Table

*The Best 1001
Short, Easy Recipes*

1001 Slow Cooker Recipes

*1001 Short, Easy,
Inexpensive Recipes*

1001 Fast Easy Recipes

1001 Community Recipes

Easy Slow Cooker Cookbook

*Busy Woman's
Slow Cooker Recipes*

*Busy Woman's
Quick & Easy Recipes*

Easy Diabetic Recipes

365 Easy Soups and Stews

365 Easy Chicken Recipes

365 Easy One-Dish Recipes

365 Easy Soup Recipes

365 Easy Vegetarian Recipes

365 Easy Casserole Recipes

365 Easy Pasta Recipes

365 Easy Slow Cooker Recipes

*Leaving Home Cookbook
and Survival Guide*

Essential 3-4-5 Ingredient Recipes

*The Ultimate Cooking
with 4 Ingredients*

Easy Cooking with 5 Ingredients

*The Best of Cooking
with 3 Ingredients*

*4-Ingredient Recipes
for 30-Minute Meals*

Cooking with Beer

The Pennsylvania Cookbook

The California Cookbook

Best-Loved New England Recipes

Best-Loved Canadian Recipes

*Best-Loved Recipes from
the Pacific Northwest*

*Easy Slow Cooker Recipes
(with Photos)*

Cool Smoothies (with Photos)

Easy Cupcakes (with Photos)

Easy Soup Recipes (with Photos)

*Classic Tex-Mex and
Texas Cooking*

Best-Loved Southern Recipes

Classic Southwest Cooking

Miss Sadie's Southern Cooking

*Classic Pennsylvania
Dutch Cooking*

*Healthy Cooking
with 4 Ingredients*

*Trophy Hunters'
Wild Game Cookbook*

Recipe Keeper

Simple Old-Fashioned Baking

Quick Fixes with Cake Mixes

*Kitchen Keepsakes & More
Kitchen Keepsakes*

Cookbook 25 Years

Texas Longhorn Cookbook

Gifts for the Cookie Jar

All New Gifts for the Cookie Jar

The Big Bake Sale Cookbook

Easy One-Dish Meals

Easy Potluck Recipes

Easy Casseroles

Easy Desserts

Sunday Night Suppers

Easy Church Suppers

365 Easy Meals

*Gourmet Cooking
with 5 Ingredients*

Muffins In A Jar

A Little Taste of Texas

A Little Taste of Texas II

**cookbook
resources** LLC

www.cookbookresources.com
Your Ultimate Source for Easy Cookbooks